Fans Love Reading
Choose Your Own Adventure®!

"This book made me want to go to Nepal
on ALL the adventures."

Sam Cady, Age 5

D0473712

"The demand for these books never really
abated and you have made this children's
librarian's dream come true."

**Marge Loch-Wouters,
Menasha Public Library, Menasha WI**

"We have had these books in our library ever
since their first publishing. They have
never gone out of demand."

**Jean Closz, Blount County
Public Library, Maryville TN**

Watch for these titles coming up in the

CHOOSE YOUR OWN ADVENTURE®

Dragonlarks™ series

Ask your bookseller for books you have missed
or visit us at cyoa.com to learn more.

YOUR VERY OWN ROBOT
by R. A. Montgomery

INDIAN TRAIL
by R. A. Montgomery

CARAVAN
by R. A. Montgomery

THE HAUNTED HOUSE
by R. A. Montgomery

MORE TITLES COMING SOON!

www.cyoa.com

CHOOSE YOUR OWN ADVENTURE®

CARAVAN

BY R.A. MONTGOMERY

A DRAGONLARK BOOK

Caravan © 1987 R. A. Montgomery
Warren, Vermont. All Rights Reserved.

Artwork, design, and revised text © 2007 Chooseco, LLC,
Waitsfield, Vermont. All Rights Reserved.

Illustrated by: Keith Newton
Book design: Stacey Hood, Big Eyedea Visual Design

For information regarding permission, write to:

CHOOSECO
P.O. Box 46
Waitsfield, Vermont 05673
www.cyoa.com

A DRAGONLARK BOOK

ISBN: 1-933390-54-9
EAN: 978-1-933390-54-3

Published simultaneously in the United States and Canada

Printed in China

0 9 8 7 6 5 4 3 2 1

To Gordon, We love ya.

A DRAGONLARK BOOK

READ THIS FIRST!!!

WATCH OUT!
THIS BOOK IS DIFFERENT
than every book you've ever read.

Don't believe me?

Have you ever read a book that was about YOU?

This book is!

YOU get to choose what happens next
—and even how the story will end.

DON'T READ THIS BOOK FROM
THE FIRST PAGE TO THE LAST.

Read until you reach a choice.
Turn to the page of the choice you like best.
If you don't like the end you reach, just start over!

"You cannot go. You are too young!"

"Father said I could, Mother. He said so," you reply.

Your mother laughs and tugs on your ear. "He said you could go when you are old enough. That is many years from now, child."

You look out the door of your house and see your father loading two shaggy yaks and three ponies with supplies and goods. He is packing for the long trip from your home in Lhasa, the capital of Tibet, to the plains of India. Yak wool and salt from Tibet and silk from China are traded for tea and spices from India.

The caravan route is long and dangerous. The caravan will have to cross the great Himalayan Mountains to get to India. The weather is bad all year round, and rocks often fall from the high mountains.

Sometimes bandits attack the caravans and rob them of their goods.

Turn to page 2 and then on to page 4.

Tibet

Nepal

India

China

Kathmandu

Great Himalaya Range

4

This year, 1696, you have decided to go—even if your parents say no. You know it will be tricky hiding from your father, for he will be on the caravan and has sharp eyes. But you are ready to take the risk.

"Go finish your lessons. Then you can help your father with the last bit of packing before he leaves. Hurry, child." Your mother has turned her back. She is busy making a list of goods to be traded in India. She is also writing down what spices your father will bring home.

You open your books, but you do not study. Instead you look at the traders who are joining the caravan. They are almost ready to go.

Should I join them tonight? you wonder, watching your father load the last bundles.

If you decide to ask your mother and father once more if you can go, turn to page 10.

If you decide to join the caravan that night, turn to page 20.

"Child, I need someone to help me on the caravan. I am old and the trip is long, but I must return to India. Will you be my helper? You will earn much good from this work. Much good."

"Yes, sir. I would be proud to help you. What would you like me to do for you now?" you answer.

He wrinkles up his face and stares at you. Finally he says, "You can either beg for our evening meal or set about finding a place for us to sleep."

If you decide to beg for an evening meal, turn to page 22.

If you search for a place to sleep, turn to page 27.

When you tell Anuradha you'll come along, she answers, "You are brave to join me. There are reports of bandits ahead. Large bands of them. I hope you ride fast. My beasts are loaded with the most beautiful Chinese silks the world has ever seen. Now keep a sharp eye."

Go on to the next page.

You nod and grip the reins of the stocky Tibetan pony that Anuradha has given you. The two of you ride off ahead of the caravan. You wrap a brightly colored scarf about your face so that your father will not know it is you. Each day you are the eyes and ears of the caravan, reporting at night what you saw and what dangers lie ahead. The days fly by. Anuradha is famous in the caravan for her intelligence and bravery.

Turn to page 33.

There is no time to wake Sangee. He is a heavy sleeper, and he will want to wake others, you decide. It's best to go quietly by yourself. It isn't far, you think, and you'll be safe.

Moments later you are in the shadows of the high mountains. The music draws you on and on. You pick your way carefully through huge boulders. Then you reach the edge of a river covered with snow and ice.

The light is beyond a glacier, higher up on the rock and snow. You walk carefully now, afraid that you will fall into a crack in the ice.

Turn to page 28.

You're about to ask your mother again when your father appears in the doorway. "Mother, child. We must talk. Come here," he says to you. He has a serious look on his face.

"Chodak says he cannot go with me. His sister is ill. He must stay here. So, I think it is time you came on the caravan to help." He looks at you. Fear and excitement rush through you. This is your chance!

"Are you ready?" he asks.

"Yes, Father, I am. May I bring my friend Sangee? He is a good helper."

"Yes, he can come. Let us go then. Do you agree, my beloved wife?" your father asks.

Your mother nods sadly. She will miss you.

Turn to page 44.

That night while you eat around the fire, Anuradha speaks to you and the others. The night is cold, and the stars shine fiercely in the sky.

"Here is where we cross to India. The Kilik Pass will lead us to the Hunza River. The pass is not too difficult, but the river gorges are steep and dangerous. Let us ask that our journey will be safe. Hold hands now, and let fear run away from us."

Turn to page 25.

When you reach the camp, you find camels, yaks, and wiry ponies tied to stakes near some round, brightly colored tents. Smoke from the cooking fires fills the air. People stay close to the fires for warmth as they drink buttered tea and eat roasted wheat and barley. You sneak up to one group. Suddenly you feel a strong hand on your shoulder.

Go on to the next page.

"Well, what do we have here?"

You turn and stare up into the face of a tall woman. She smiles.

"Do you want to join my party in the caravan, young one?" she asks. "Are you a hard worker? We start early in the morning."

If you decide to join the woman's party,
turn to page 19.

If you decide to find other work, turn to page 49.

"Sangee, wake up! Wake up, Sangee," you say, shaking him. He turns over, wraps his blanket tightly around his body, and tries to push you away.

"Sangee! The mountain spirits are here. We must see them. Come! They will bring us good luck, good fortune. Please, Sangee."

Finally Sangee wakes. He listens to the music and watches the light. It is strange, you think, that no one else in the caravan has noticed these things. Perhaps they are for only you two to witness. A special sign to both of you!

Turn to page 30.

You leap up and dash for the opening in the wall. One of the bandits hears you and rushes toward you. He grabs your sleeve.

"Help! Help!" you yell. The bandit stumbles, and your sleeve rips. You are free! You race across the open field toward where the caravan is camping.

"Bandits! Bandits!" you cry. Within minutes thirty members of the caravan are following you back to the empty house. They quickly round up the bandits.

You have saved the caravan! Even the holy man joins in the celebration of your bravery.

The End

"I am a hard worker," you answer, trying to sound older than you are.

"Well, we'll see about that," she says. "My name is Anuradha."

The next day you are put to work repacking the camels and ponies. You are one of six people who have joined Anuradha's party. At noon you hear the cries of the caravan leader and the tinkle of the bells around the animals' necks. The camels snarl loudly. The caravan has begun.

"Hey, there, young one, do you want to scout the way ahead? Or do you wish to stay here with the animals and the others?"

You look up at the smiling face of Anuradha and try to decide. It is dangerous to scout ahead of the caravan. And your father may see you—he is at the head of the caravan. But scouting ahead could be exciting.

If you decide to help with the scouting,
turn to page 6.

If you decide to stay with the animals,
turn to page 37.

As soon as it's dark you get ready to leave. Many days ago you packed what you will need on the caravan. In your pack you put clothes, yak-skin boots with wooden soles, a knife, fur hat, and a fur-lined coat. You also packed some dried apples and apricots. You know that it's smart to bring along extra food.

With the bundle over your shoulder, you slip away from home. You move along carefully in the darkness, hoping your mother doesn't spot you. Since your father is already riding on the caravan, you don't have to worry about him—yet. You stop for a moment, worried about what you are doing. Then you hurry away toward the part of town where the caravan from China is camping.

Turn to page 12.

"If you give me the bowl, I will find food for us," you say, reaching for the monk's wooden bowl. Many monks ask their helpers to ask for food for them. It is their pay for helping on the caravan.

The monk hands you the bowl and folds his robe closely about him. Then he sits cross-legged on the ground beside a pile of bundles covered with a black cloth. He nods at you and then studies his beads as he repeats ancient stories of the mountain spirits.

You head off in the direction of nearby inns.

Turn to page 40.

The next day, after the caravan safely crosses the Kilik Pass, something scary happens. In the steep river gorge a pony loses its footing. The animal and the young boy on its back almost fall into the rough water.

Once you know the boy and pony are safe, Anuradha asks the spirits of the mountain to keep all of you safe. You all pray for the safety of the caravan. The trip is not over yet—India still lies ahead.

The End

Where can I take this monk? you ask yourself. It will be cold tonight, and he will need a warm place to sleep.

You look around. Suddenly, an idea comes to you. Along the caravan route, there is an empty house. It is old and broken down, but not too far away.

You lead the monk to the house. The two of you step inside. The house is clean and empty. He sleeps. You sit on the hard floor and wait for dawn.

Near morning low voices wake you up. The monk has left. Who is talking? you wonder.

Turn to page 43.

After you make it safely across the glacier, you climb the rocky wall. The music sounds louder, and you think that you will soon reach it. The white light fills more and more of the sky until it is almost as bright as daylight.

In the distance, a voice that sounds half-human, half-animal lets out a cry. *"Aaiiii!"*

You stand still, not wanting to make any noise. Then you hear the voice again. Only this time it is louder and closer. *"Aaiiii! Aaiiiiii!"*

If you decide to run away, turn to page 34.

If you decide to stay and see what happens, turn to page 38.

Three days later you are on the other side of the mountain pass. The caravan has safely made it over the steep river gorges. This is India, and already the heat from the Indian plains brings warmth to the air.

You almost forget the music and bright lights in your excitement of a new land with new sounds and people.

But you know you'll never forget anything about this trip!

The End

Quietly you and Sangee slip out of camp. You climb a rocky trail and cross a milk-white glacier. With each step, the music sounds sweeter and the light grows brighter.

"Maybe we have discovered the home of the mountain spirits," you say to Sangee.

"We'll soon see," he answers.

Go on to the next page.

Just as you reach the far side of the glacier, boulders crash from high above. They nearly crush both of you. Sangee turns to you and asks, "Are they a warning from the hands of spirits?"

If you say, "I think they fell by chance. Let's go on," turn to page 47.

If you answer, "The boulders must be some kind of warning," turn to page 36.

You have been with the caravan for three weeks. There has been little time to think about home, except at night when you roll up in your thick blanket for sleep.

You miss your mother and younger sister and brother, but you know your father is nearby. He's right there on the caravan—even though you take care that he does not see you!

One morning you are awakened suddenly. Someone is leaning over your bedroll.

"Father! How did you find me?" you ask, surprised to see him.

"I thought you would come. I was young once, too, you know. You have worked well. Anuradha is a friend, and she speaks well of you. Welcome! It's on to India now. There you'll see elephants and tigers, palaces and maharajas, things you never dreamed of."

The End

You turn to run, but standing behind you is a huge creature. It has the face of a man and the body of a gorilla. You bump right into it.

The creature howls with fear and runs off into the mountains. You can't believe anything that big can run so fast!

Running in the other direction, you slip and slide across the glacier, stumbling down the rocky trail to camp.

Turn to page 53.

"We must turn back, Sangee," you add. "The spirits are angry. The next boulders will not miss us."

Sangee nods, and the two of you turn to leave. And you're just in time! There's a loud noise behind you. You look back at the mountain. Two more big boulders have fallen from above. They've landed right where you and your friend were standing!

Next to you Sangee shivers. "Let's get out of here!" you cry, grabbing his arm. And the two of you race away toward camp—and safety.

The End

"I like working with the ponies. I'll stay back here," you say.

The animals need a lot of care. Their heavy packs are taken off each afternoon, and then they are tied to stakes to stop them from roaming.

Turn to page 39.

You stay still. Minutes seem frozen in time and space. No more sounds fill the night air. The music stops. The bright white light dims and then is gone.

You soon grow cold and tired. Quietly you return to camp.

Turn to page 29.

Next you must feed them, check their hooves for cuts, and make sure their legs are firm. Any cuts you find are dressed so that they heal quickly.

Finally, you have crossed the Great Plain of Central Asia. Now you are at the foot of the Pamir Mountains, part of the great Himalayan chain.

Turn to page 11.

At one of the inns you find a kind woman. She heaps a wooden bowl with food. You hurry back to the monk. He sits in the same spot.

"Here, I have brought food," you say.

He raises his head and opens his eyes. They shine with a bright light. He smiles and speaks: "It is my time to go from this life. Your kindness on my last day on this earth warms me for my journey. Take this as my gift to you."

He places the string of beads in your hands. Then he closes his eyes. Life passes from him.

"What shall I do now?" you ask out loud.

"I will help you, child," says your father, who is now standing beside you. "Your kindness to this old man has earned you reward. You may come with me on the caravan. You have shown that you are old enough."

The End

"We will rob the caravan when it is farther from Lhasa," you hear a man say, "Will your friends be ready?"

"My friends are waiting now in the hills," another man answers. "At noon I will give them the signal."

The men are bandits who plan to rob the caravan! You hold your breath, trying not to make a sound.

You hear the men rolling out some blankets. "We have time for a nap," one of the bandits says. You must warn the caravan right away. There's a big hole in the wall to your left. You could sneak through it now, but maybe it'd be safer to wait until the men have fallen asleep.

If you try to escape right away, turn to page 16.

If you wait until the bandits are asleep, turn to page 50.

Three weeks later you and the caravan have traveled beyond the plains of Tibet. You are high in the Pamir Mountains, and India lies on the other side.

One night as you sit in camp, you hear a sound and see a bright light beyond the ring of campfires. The sound is clear and sweet—like music. The light is like a star fallen to earth.

You want to explore them, but leaving the caravan may be dangerous.

If you decide to explore on your own, turn to page 8.

If you decide to wake your friend Sangee, turn to page 15.

"There are always rockfalls in the mountains," you say, trying to sound brave. "Let's go."

After a hard scramble you reach a ledge. When you look down, the sight before you is magnificent! There you see hundreds of figures, each shimmering brightly like sunlight on an icy mountain. The figures are dressed in jewels. Beams of light shine from their heads and hands and feet. As they move, music fills the air.

"It is the dance of life. I've heard of it from the elders," Sangee says.

You watch until dawn. With the first ray of sunlight the figures vanish and the music stops.

"Sangee, we've seen something special," you say to your friend.

"I know," he replies. The two of you return to camp in silence, amazed at what you saw.

The End

"No, I think I'll find other work," you say.

"Well, on with you then," she answers. "There is much to do." She walks back to the fire and sits down.

You come across an old, weathered, bent man. He is white-haired and dressed in maroon robes. In his hands are a long string of beads. He must be a monk who travels with the caravans. Perhaps he is a type of doctor.

Turn to page 5.

While you wait for the bandits to fall asleep, your nose starts to itch. You are afraid you will sneeze! But luckily you don't.

A few minutes later you hear the bandits snoring. You creep out of the house and head for where the caravan is camping.

The first person you see is Anuradha. You tell her all about the men.

"You're a good one," she says, clapping you on the back. "I'll take care of this."

By noon the bandits are in jail. Anuradha turns to you when the caravan starts up. "You have saved the caravan," she says. "Your bravery will be rewarded. You and the holy man will sit beside me on the caravan. Together we will lead the way to India."

You can't wait to get there!

The End

Back at camp you tell your story to the others, but no one believes you. They laugh and say you dreamed it. Only you know what you saw—the Abominable Snowman that's said to live in the Pamir Mountains. What about the light and music? you wonder all the time. Maybe they came from the Abominable Snowman, maybe from other mountain spirits. Perhaps someday you will learn the answer.

The End

ABOUT THE AUTHOR

At the Temple of Literature and National University
(Van Mieu-Quoc Tu Giam) in Hanoi, Vietnam

R. A. MONTGOMERY has hiked in the Himalayas, climbed mountains in Europe, scuba-dived in Central America, and worked in Africa. He lives in France in the winter, travels frequently to Asia, and calls Vermont home. Montgomery graduated from Williams College and attended graduate school at Yale University and NYU. His interests include macro-economics, geo-politics, mythology, history, mystery novels, and music. He has two grown sons, a daughter-in-law, and two granddaughters. His wife, Shannon Gilligan, is an author and noted interactive game designer. Montgomery feels that the new generation of people under 15 is the most important asset in our world.

**For games, activities and other fun stuff,
or to write to R. A. Montgomery,
visit us online at CYOA.com**

CREDITS

This book was brought to life by a great group of people. R. A. Montgomery thought long and hard about how his adventures could be restored for today's reader, and brought this manuscript into the Internet age. Just down the hall, Shannon Gilligan took on the complex role of Publisher. Gordon Troy performed the legal pirouettes that result in proper trademark and copyright protections. Stacey Hood at Big Eyedea Visual Design in Swan Valley, Montana, was responsible for layout and design. Melissa Bounty offered editorial harmony wherever possible. Betti LoVulle gracefully commanded Operations, and Jason Geller took control of National Sales. Adrienne Cady came onboard as Publisher's Assistant. Kris Town and Robin Haggerman checked and rechecked all the numbers in Accounting, and Jim Wallace dotted the i's and crossed the t's as our Proofreader.

Illustrator: Keith Newton began his art career in the theater as a set painter. Having talent and a strong desire to paint portraits, he moved to New York and studied fine art at the Art Students League. Keith has won numerous awards in art such as The Grumbacher Gold Medallion and Salmagundi Award for Pastel. He soon began illustrating and was hired by Disney Feature Animation where he worked on such films as *Pocahontas* and *Mulan* as a background artist. Keith also designed color models for sculptures at Disney Animal Kingdom and has animated commercials for Euro Disney. Today, Keith Newton freelances from his home and teaches entertainment illustration at The College for Creative Studies in Detroit. He is married and has two daughters.

Original Fans Love Reading
Choose Your Own Adventure®!

The books let readers remix their own stories—and face the consequences. Kids race to discover lost civilizations, navigate black holes, and go in search of the Yeti, revamped for the 21st century!
Wired Magazine

I love CYOA—I missed CYOA! I've been keeping my fingers as bookmarks on pages 45, 16, 32, and 9 all these years, just to keep my options open.
Madeline, 20

Reading a CYOA book was more like playing a video game on my treasured Nintendo® system. I'm pretty sure the multiple plot twists of *The Lost Jewels of Nabooti* are forever stored in some part of my brain.
The Fort Worth Star Telegram

How I miss you, CYOA! I only have a small shelf left after my mom threw a bunch of you away in a yard sale—she never did understand.
Travis Rex, 26

I LOVE CYOA BOOKS! I have read them since I was a small child. I am so glad to hear they are going back into print! You have just made me the happiest person in the world!
Carey Walker, 27